Full-Color Charted Designs

by Anne Orr

Dover Publications, Inc.
New York

Copyright © 1984 by Anne Callahan.
All rights reserved under Pan American and International Copyright Conventions.

Published in Canada by General Publishing Company, Ltd., 30 Lesmill Road, Don Mills, Toronto, Ontario.

Published in the United Kingdom by Constable and Company, Ltd., 10 Orange Street, London WC2H 7EG.

Full-Color Charted Designs is a new work, first published by Dover Publications, Inc., in 1984 through the interest and with the permission of Anne Orr's granddaughter, Miss Anne Callahan, who supplied the handpainted originals from which the charts in this book were reproduced.

Manufactured in the United States of America
Dover Publications, Inc., 31 East 2nd Street, Mineola, N.Y. 11501

Library of Congress Cataloging in Publication Data

Orr, Anne Champe.
 Full-color charted designs.

(Dover needlework series)
 1. Needlework—Patterns. I. Title.
TT753.O783 1984 746.44′041 84-4154
ISBN 0-486-24732-5 (pbk.)

Publisher's Note

The popularity of charted and other needlework designs can be traced to the sixteenth century with the publication of collections of charts for embroidery, lace and weaving, and by 1800 more than 150 pattern books had appeared in print in Britain and Europe. In the United States the last quarter of the nineteenth century and the first quarter of the twentieth century witnessed several influences which were to enhance the quality and sophistication of professionally drafted charts and designs. Expansion and development in thread manufacture along with the ever-growing emphasis on print advertising as a vehicle for nationwide marketing were able to bring the designs of talented designers into almost every household. Until the second half of the nineteenth century men had dominated needlework design, but with the establishment of higher education for women this hegemony waned.

Anne Champe Orr was a prolific and well-loved American designer of popular needlework who emphasized quality and versatility in her designs. Author of almost 100 books of needlework patterns in the years between 1914 and 1945, Anne Orr also was the needlework editor of *Good Housekeeping* for 21 years. Her best-known charted designs were for embroidery and filet crochet, but she also designed for knitting, crochet, tatting, appliqué and quiltmaking. Her counted-thread drafts may be used in a variety of needlework techniques such as needlepoint, mosaic crochet, petit point, beadwork, darned-net lace and canvas embroidery. Primarily, Anne Orr was a conceptualizer who intended artisans to adapt her charted designs to their own imaginative purposes.

Dover has published three previous books by Anne Orr which are part of the Dover Needlework Series: *Crochet Designs of Anne Orr* (0-486-23621-8), *Anne Orr's Charted Designs* (0-486-23704-4) and *Favorite Charted Designs of Anne Orr, Including 119 in Full Color* (0-486-24484-9). This present work contains designs that were hand-painted at the Anne Orr Studio in Nashville, Tennessee, and were recently uncovered by Anne Orr's granddaughter, Anne Callahan. Most have probably never been published before.

Because they show Anne Orr at the height of her ability as a designer and colorist, it was Miss Callahan's wish that they be made available to the many needleworkers who for years have admired Mrs. Orr's work. Dover Publications is thus privileged to offer a "new" collection with a charming variety of compositions: designs which show animals, people, landscapes and, of course, florals, including two beautiful designs for borders.

We would like to acknowledge the use of information in the introductions to two previous Anne Orr needlework books provided by Rachel Maines, the President of the Center for the History of American Needlework in Ambridge, Pennsylvania, which was incorporated in this Publisher's Note.

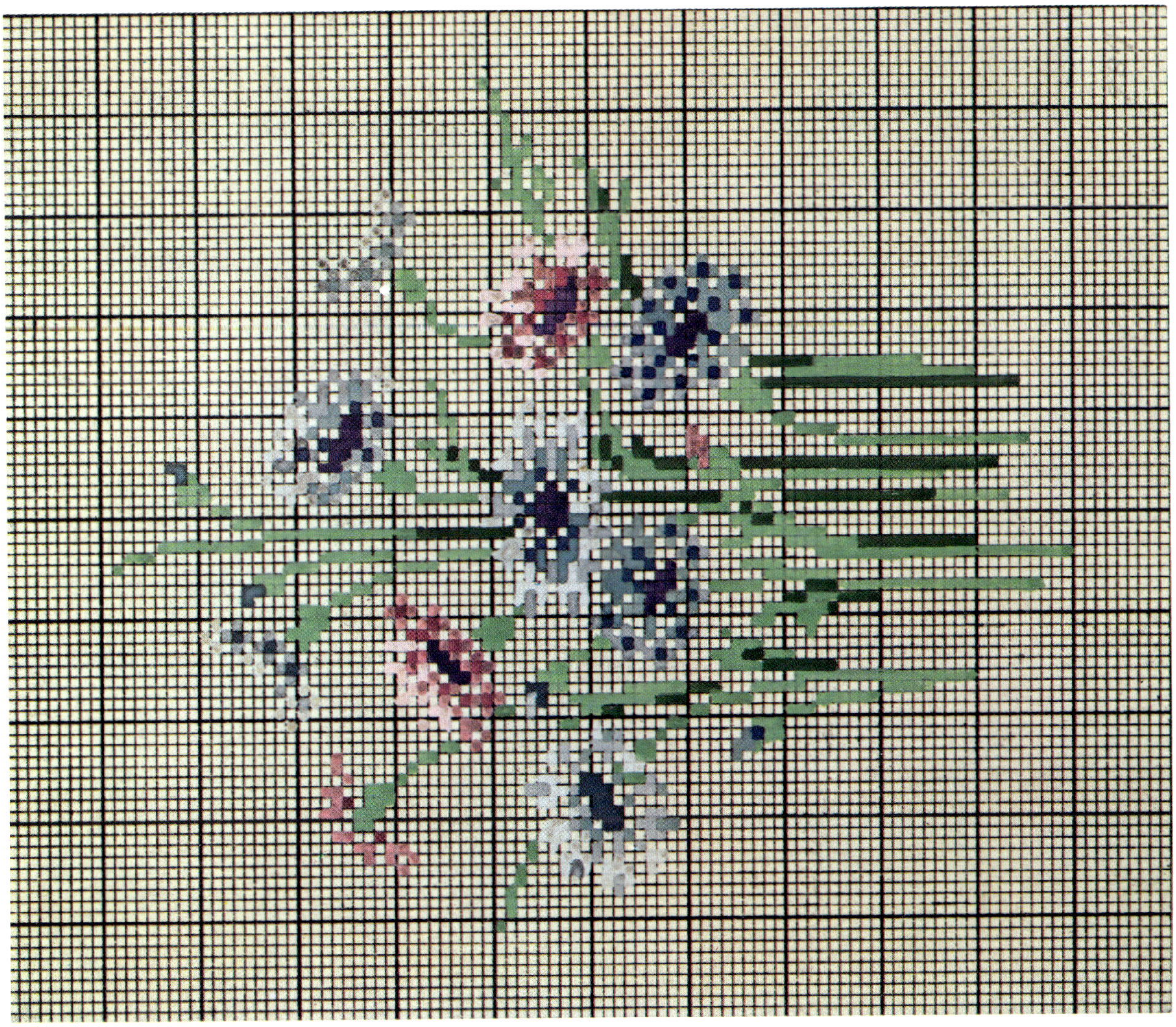

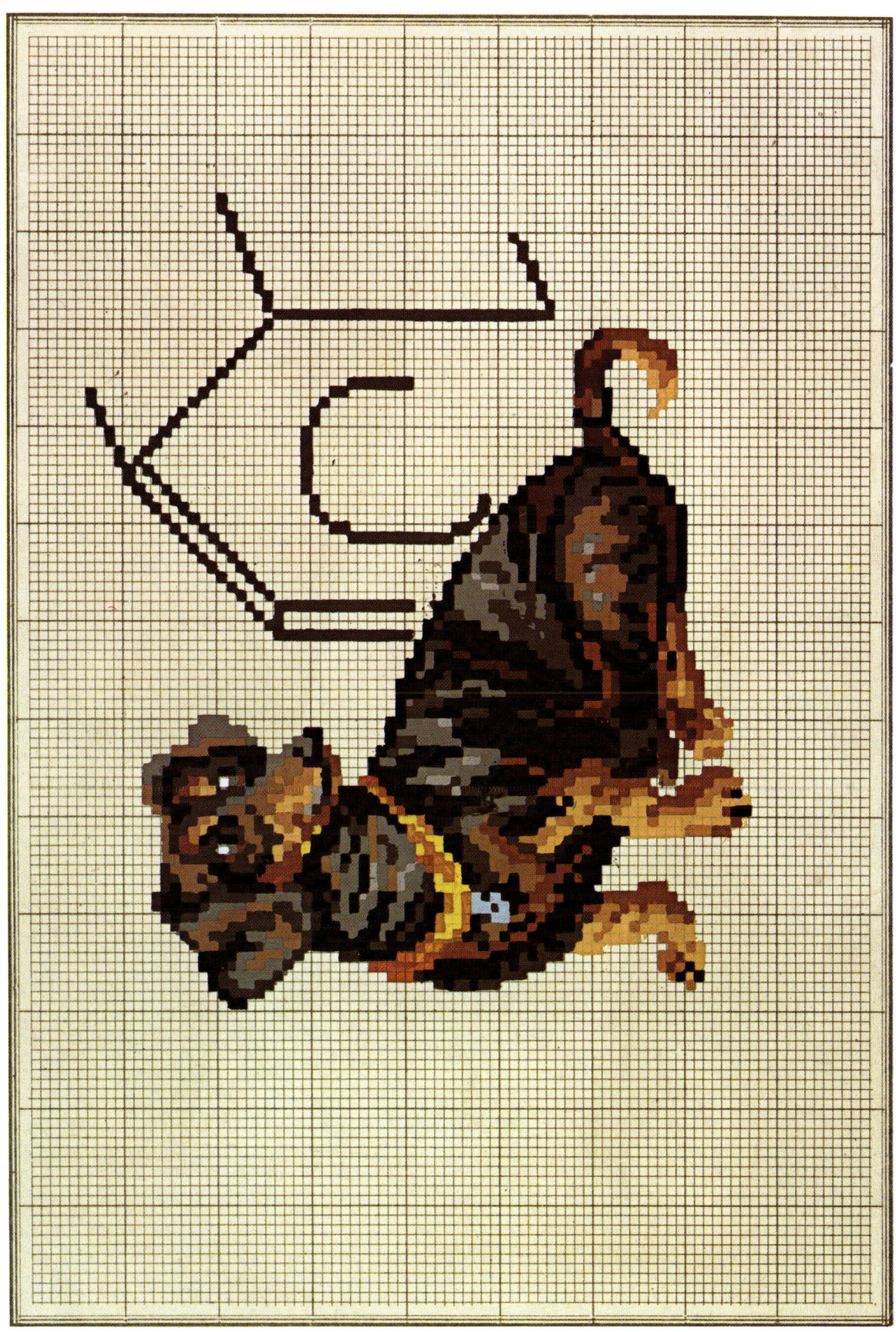